Interludes

...in between those lines

Sunanda Sheily

BookLeaf Publishing

India | USA | UK

Made with ❤ on the BookLeaf Publishing Platform
www.bookleafpub.in
www.bookleafpub.com

To my kids, Shreenidhi and Shreevardhan...

Acknowledgement

As I hold my first book in my hands, I find it impossible not to reflect on the incredible people who have supported me through every step of this journey.

To my parents, whose love and belief in me have been the bedrock of my existence—thank you for your unwavering support. You've always encouraged me to follow my heart, never questioning my choices, and always standing by me, no matter what.

To my brother, Subhro and my sister-in-law, Vidushi—my rock and my critic—thank you for being the one who pushes me to be better, even when it's hard to hear. Your honest feedback and constant presence have given me the courage to evolve, while your unshakable support has kept me anchored. You have been my strength in moments of doubt, and for that, I am forever grateful.

To Nishu didi, my first true inspiration. Watching you write with such dedication opened my eyes to the beauty of words. It was your passion and commitment that ignited I my own path as a writer.

A special mention to Swati, whose unwavering support during my maternity days was nothing short of incredible. Despite managing your own toddler, you stood by me every step of the way, offering strength and love beyond what I could have imagined. Your commitment to my writing matched your care for me—extraordinary and relentless. You motivated me to never stop writing, even suggested that I send voice notes when I couldn't put pen to paper. Your faith in me and my work has never wavered, and I can never be grateful enough for your constant encouragement. You are truly one of a kind.

To Amu—my irreplaceable friend from our engineering days. You've been that iron lady who patiently endured my poetry, becoming my first ever audience. I'll always remember those late-night "intellectual" bonding sessions when everyone else was engaged in debates, and I was lost in my diary, scribbling down my thoughts. With each poem I completed, I couldn't wait to share it with you, often springing up with excitement and exclaiming, "It's done!" You were always there, even when my readings were untimely and out of context. I hope, after all these years, you curse me a little less for those moments today!

I want to express my deepest gratitude to my incredible friends Pranav, Soban, Jyoti, and Neeta. You are the steady anchors in my life, the ones who've weathered every storm with me. Through my mood swings, the chaos of my thoughts, and unpredictable tides of emotions, you've remained by my side with unfaltering patience and care. You've listened to my 3 a.m. rants, celebrated my joys, shared my sorrows, and stood beside me with no expectation other than friendship. You've embraced my flaws with open arms, never once questioning or judging. Your love is the kind that asks for nothing yet gives everything. In ways big and small, your presence has made this journey of life so much richer. Words fail to capture the depth of my gratitude, but know that I am forever indebted to you for being the pillars I can always lean on.

I am deeply grateful to all those whose paths I have crossed, no matter the time or space we've shared. I firmly believe that every meeting holds a purpose, and perhaps, in the unfolding of my poems, you were the very reason.

This book is a reflection of all of you—your love, your patience, and your unwavering support. Thank you for being a part of my journey.

Preface

I have always been an introvert—most of the time, yes, I am an introvert. Writing has been my only outlet for expression, as I've never quite managed to convey myself in any other way. I've often stumbled through my actions, struggling to articulate my feelings in the moment. As a result, I've let people, opportunities, and even love slip away simply because I couldn't find the words. Regret serves no purpose now, but at the very least I have writing—a means to excavate the hidden, unspoken, and often untouched emotions. Through poetry, I've been able to distill a fraction of the countless thoughts that race through my mind, often at the most unearthly hours.

Poetry, for me, is like a quiet sanctuary, a secluded corner of my world where I feel most myself, untouched, unguarded, and free from the weight of others' judgments. It's a place where I lose track of whether I am within the poetry or the poetry is within me. It's where my thoughts, emotions, and experiences find their truest voice.

This collection of poems is the culmination of many quiet moments, late-night musings, and personal reflections. Each word is a reflection of a journey, both deeply personal and universal, woven from the threads of love, loss, hope, and resilience.

As you turn these pages, I invite you to embark on this journey with me. Let these poems serve as a mirror, a window, or a companion—whatever you need them to be in this moment. May they offer you as much comfort and understanding as they have offered me in the writing.

Thank you for taking the time to read my words. This book is as much yours as it is mine.

You Hold...

I hold
hold eons
eons of moments
moments so dense
dense with interludes
interludes of desolation
desolation of your absence
absence longing for gratification
gratification of fulfillment
fulfillment of each minutiae
minutiae drenched in love
love in eternal being
being in sheltering arms
arms of you
You hold...

Cosmic Journey...

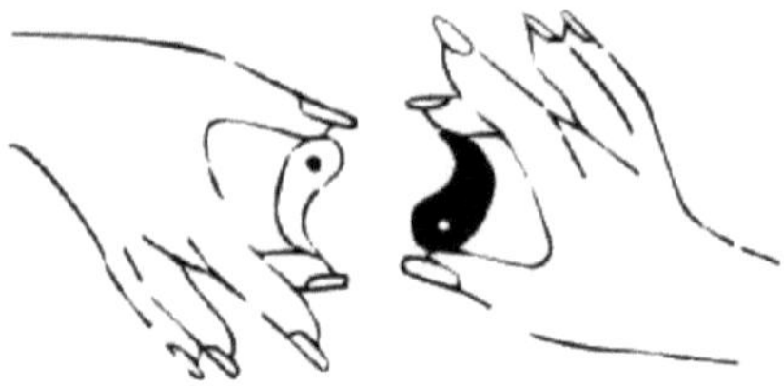

At the core of the sun, light first gleams,
Vast and radiant, awareness streams.
The supreme source, its rays ignite,
Ablaze! Pure, eternal, bright.
Within this boundless, cosmic hearth,
Life, finally, takes its birth.
In stars, planets, on moons and galaxies
Quasars, comets, and celestial taxies.
Divine order of cosmic dance,
Heavenly beings hold their stance.
Creative kiln, thus whispers,
Echoes neighboring fond wisters.

To Mercury, the essence takes flight,
Refines conscious with insight.
Swift and nimble, small yet bright,
Wisdom awakens, conscience alight.
From Mercury's lap, the seed of sense,

Travels to Venus, meets elegance!

In Venus's glow, intelligence shines,
Polished and pure, where melody chimes.
Soaked in artistry, elegance-dressed,
The enchantress is ready for her quest
Enlightened with the language of love,
Primed for the next cosmic trove.

To Earth, where life begins to sing,
And matter joins in a harmonious ring.
Among people, it finds its space,
Tasting pleasures, yet leaves no trace.
A soul unbound, free to roam,
It mingles, yet stays far from home.
In Earth's embrace, it charts its way,
Yet moves with wisdom, far from sway.

To Mars, where courage fiercely burns,
Knowledge with valor, a power it earns.
The pen is mightier than a sword, it learns.
Bejeweled with conscience and elegance,
Awareness attains conformity,
Mettle and grit fortify resonance.

Next, to Jupiter's expansive gaze,
Where wisdom sprawls, a guiding maze.
The mentor's eyes, the truth to find,
The cosmic law, in all its mind.

To Saturn's rings, where karma spins,
The weight of deeds, the hand of fate.
A balance struck, the past unveiled,
In Saturn's grasp, the truth is told.

Then Uranus, ancient and wide,
Holds memory's vault, the cosmic tide.
Through time's fluid stretch, it guards the key,
Eternal truths, from now to infinity.

To Neptune's depths, where dreams reside,
Reflections dance on the ocean's tide.
In mystic waters, secrets sleep,
The vast unknown, forever deep.

Finally, to Pluto's glacial ground,
Truth resides safe in a timeless bound,
Reveal mysteries, profound and bold,
In silence, the deepest secrets are told.

Through this eternal, ceaseless sweep,
Knowledge flows, vast and deep.
Changing hands, from nascent raw,
Awareness to wisdom, to conscious,
Flowing abound in galactic law.
In this realm, or beyond the unseen,
Bound by the laws of all that has been,
What we perceive or stories retold,
The Cosmic Journey, nevertheless, unfolds...

Lux

Amidst the dynamics of improbability,
where space and time
weave in random flux,
one that gives goosebumps,
in moments so uncanny,
lies your source of all that Lux!

What Love is Not....

I searched for love's true meaning,
but found only words—
unconditional, unseen, eternal, divine—
promises tangled in the grip of ambition.
I delved deeper,
and there, a storm of voices rose,
whispering, "Let us fall,
let us fathom this depth,
for life is more than just numbers and rules."
So they fell,
never to rise again,
believing all was fair,
that wisdom bloomed from the fall.
They sank into hearts,
filled with fleeting illusions,
as if no force could tear them apart.

Then, in stillness,
the peak arrived,
as destiny softly tapped,
revealing a fragile thread
within a tapestry unraveled.
And now they cry,
"Who will rescue us?"
But did they ever ask themselves?
Did they pause,
glance inward,
or reach out when it mattered most?
Stop.
Pouring from an empty well
only sparks a flame—
one that consumes what remains of your spirit.
In my search to define love,
I traced its absence,
and found what love is not.
Love is not the words you shout,
nor the heights it promises to lift you to.
It is not found in myths,
or relics of the past.

Love resides in the quiet corners
of your own unbroken being,
inseparable, whole,
and ever true.

Let me Be in my Dreams...

On a frosty winter's morning,
when soft vermilion hues leap
from the clouds to peek,
and the gentle tinkle of porcelain
stirs my sleep.
My lazy eyes flutter open,
to hands offering a tray,
the rich aroma of coffee,
a dewdrop perched upon a vase,
dresses for a sunny day.
His smile, a bloom on parted lips,
the fragrance of his being,
drenches me in ecstasy,
tuning my heart to sing.

Through the coniferous woods we wander,
among tall, snow-laden trees,
while the afternoon sun, like golden threads,
weaves through nature's masterpiece.
Our mortal forms dissolve,
lost in the mercy of a breeze
that stirs hearts
as if touched by Cupid's hand,
Our fingers entwined in a seamless helix.
My cold cheeks resting
on his warm, steady chest,
the rhythm of his heart,
sending my pulse to its highest crest.
Evening snowfall lights the hearth,
candles and lamps flicker,
dimmed beneath
the power of his embrace.
Desires burn with quiet intensity,
mercury slipping from tip to toe,
spilling from the bowl,
spreading like molten diamonds
across velvet turf,
until all is laid low in their final,
shimmering glow.
Poor red chiffon

knows neither joy nor regret,
held captive by his touch,
while the quills and pillows,
still untouched,
wait patiently
to witness what remains unsaid,
Let me stay within my dreams...

Mirror

Scared feet,
In time's relentless beat,
Climb peaks, ford the streams,
From scorching days to gentle dreams,
And through the moon's soft silver light,
They wander on through starry night.

Learning starts,
Destiny, with patient heart,
Weaves, sighs, and grins,
For she knows what truth begins.
This boundless light will lead them all
To rest in peace, at fate's soft call,
A bed unshakable, firm and sure,
In a world where questions cease to endure.

The doyen warns with steady voice,
"Beware the bends, you have no choice,
For the liquid path that leads to bliss
Is never straight, it swerves, it twists..."

Well-decorated feet, camouflaged,
With hearts full of hope, yet quite distraught,
Pack their bags and pull their socks,
Wave goodbye with fleeting knocks.
The journey starts, the turf slips by,
The glimmering, mysterious sky,
Calls them forth to what's unknown,
To realms where light and shadows roam.

Heart and mind, torn in strife,
Prepare themselves to face their life,
With courage firm and spirits bright,
To battle on through endless night.
Oh, what a feeling, oh, what grace,
A peace that fills this empty space—
On clouds they soar, on seas they glide,
On roads they walk with hearts open wide,
But was it all a dream they seek,
A fleeting truth too soft to speak?

The conclusion, clear and bright,
The aqueous is the guiding light,
It grants the stillness Nirvana's hold,
A reflector to the soul, untold.
It's all around, it reflects the shine—
A love so pure, so undefined,
A faith so firm, it stands through time,
A power that's quiet, yet sublime.
Even the darkest, burning desire,
Finds its place in aqueous fire.
The aqueous is karma's hand,
It scatters seeds across the land,
It nurtures cycles, old and new,
It shows the depths of what is true.
It shows what lies in ether's sea,
The front, the rear, what's meant to be,
In symbiosis, all align,
The aqueous projects the inner shine.

The aqueous is omnipotent,
A mirror to what's never spent,
It shows the world and all its face,
But also truth in every trace,
It turns the inside out,

both whole and split,
And all the mysteries
of life, with grit.

The Kinds

Sea of Kinds
Individualities at the helm,
Fishes of self,
Swim, overwhelmed.
Blocks of ice
Arrest life and decay,
No fire, no chaos,
No passion, no sway,
Love or dismay.
Caught and taken,
Are traps that possess,
Caught in moments,
Taken for granted—left to assess.
Fathom the seas outside,
Courage calls, uncharted,
Yet the deepest mines within,
Ain't for the faint-hearted.

Nirvana? Why?

Why this quest for the heavenly,
The starry, the galactical,
The longing for what's unreachable?
Why this thirst for intoxication,
For trance, for numbness, for sleep?

While here, in the now,
Why turn a blind eye to pain,
To the struggle, or tears for loss?

While here, in the now,
Why not dream of the local,
As common, as simple,
As earthly, as love?

Why reach for the distant, the grand,
When beauty blooms at our feet, so close at hand?
Why wander the stars, lost and afar,
When truth is alive in the pulse of who we are?

We search for peace beyond the sky,
But is it not here, where our hearts lie?
In the mundane, the simple, the raw,
There exists a joy beyond all we saw.

For in the depths of each passing day,
There's a truth waiting to light our way.
No need for far-off lands to find,
When Nirvana resides in the heart and mind.

So ask, in the quiet of your mind,
Is peace not here, where in hind?
Nirvana? Why?

Synergy

A streak of light,
A glimpse of beloved's sight,
Miles apart, no mapped design,
Yet, in essence, souls align.

In a dance of time, a perfect swing,
I pause, wondering what it might bring—
Until, like dawn, a clue unfolds,
A truth so deep, a story told.

It's timeless, universal, and pure,
A rhythm eternal, yet ever sure:
To give love, selfless and divine,
Is to touch the stars, where hearts align.
To receive it back, like winter's sun,
A warmth that melts all fears, undone.

Love, with buoyant, soaring grace,
Waves of frequencies fill empty space.
These frequencies matter,
They're real, they're near,
They carry your whispers,
Your joy, your fear.
They bind you to the one you adore,
And nourish your "love diet" evermore.

Frequencies guide your heart's silent plea,
Shaping your wishes, your dreams to be,
They rise and fall, like tides of fate,
Calling to you, never too late.
They bind and lose, they find and lead,
In quiet moments, they plant the seed,
A flawless connection, so serene,
A bond so deep, forever keen,
Two hearts entwined, like stars above,
Shining together in boundless love,
Of all transforming energy,
The union pure, wild, and free,
A perfect rhythm,
An endless synergy.

Memory (loss)

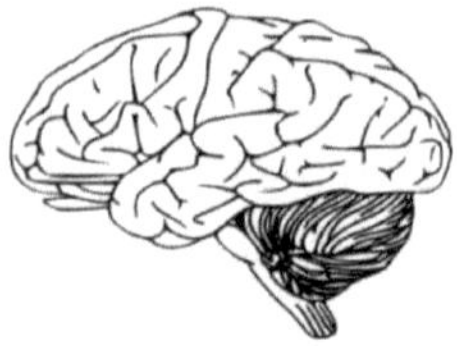

Every word that wounds the soul,
Every thought that takes its toll,
Every image that scars the heart,
Nature whispers, "Let them depart."
With its grace, so pure and deep,
It calms the storm, and lets peace sleep,
Cleansing the mind, the heart, the core,
Restoring harmony forevermore.

And yet, we call it a "disease" to forget,
When nature's healing gift resets.
In its embrace, the wounds unwind,
A tender cure for the troubled mind.
Forgetting is not a pain to bear,
Nature's way to mend and repair—
Memory loss!

Embrace of the Dark

In the stillness of night,
Where shadows sigh,
A seed stirs beneath the earth,
Hidden from sight.

In the cold, unyielding fold,
Life writes a story, until untold.
How we tremble at night's quiet call,
Silence that urges to pause, to fall.

Yet in this realm, where no life dares tread,
All growth takes root, miracles are fed.
We curse the dark, forgetting its grace—
The space where burdens unravel, find their
place.

Where sorrow is cradled, joy takes form,
Hearts are released, and spirits are warm.

Without you, darkness, where would I seek
Gentleness to heal the fractured, weak?
How would I touch the stars, distant and
sway,
If your arms didn't hold, keeping fear away?

What is light, if not a blinding flare,
A blazing flash that vanishes in air?
It dazzles the eyes, puzzles the soul,
While in your calm, we are made whole.

In your hush, we find our grace,
A peace no radiance could replace.

Without you, how'd I know true rest?
The sweet release, the quiet nest?
Where tears can fall, unbound and free,
We're healed in your sanctuary.

In your refuge, the soul finds peace,
A stillness where all burdens cease.
You are the quiet where dreams take flight,
The place where broken wings ignite.

In the dark, we find the light we crave,
And through calm, our hearts are saved.
You are the unseen strength we need,
The quiet force where we are freed.

In your embrace, all fears depart,
We are whole, restored, and sparked—
Cradled in the boundless, soothing mark,
Of the *Embrace of the Dark.*

Synapses

Bit by bit like stars,
Igniting the vast sky,
In luminous phases,
Amidst growing darkness;
Are our neurons,
Sparked by *Synapses*,
Of predominant and
Inevitable, scattered,
In the expanding consciousness.

Colors

If blood alone could claim the price of grace,
Then saffron would mark the fallen's sacred place.
True tribute lies not in red's cruel stain,
But in memories that time cannot restrain.

Peace beneath the darkened night's embrace,
Is untouched by war, by violence's trace.
Remains unbroken, steadfast and still,
A quiet strength against the world's harsh will.

If green were loved with hearts open wide,
We'd plant not just trees, but hope as our guide.
Not reopening wounds that time has sealed,
But allowing nature's balm, in silence, healed.

Trusting the blue sky, calm and true,
Lead us onward, to paths anew.
To chase the past while running ahead,
Is but a fool's errand, a road misled.
Better to focus on what lies near,
Deaf to the past, which only brings fear.
Release the ghosts, the shadows of yore,
And embrace the strength of the now, evermore.
The present is the hand that holds the key,
To unlock the peace we long to see.

Revolution is not found in tearing down,
But in lifting oneself, wearing the crown.
Focus not on the faults of another's way,
But center within, for a brighter day.
Saffron calls for surrender, pure and bright,
White whispers love that knows no night.
Green speaks of healing when we stray,
Beneath the blue, we find our way.
For hues are not just shades we behold,
But sacred messages, quiet and bold.
Each *Color* whispers truths, soft and deep—
If we look beyond, and in silence, leap.

A Rebel

In the pursuit for power,
And, vivid hues of love,
Amidst the battle of right and wrong,
Yet, when ego rises, it claims the stage—
Breathing deeply, unseen, within us.
Why, then, does the heart ache,
Wounded by its own hand?
Seeking solace in a world so vast,
When the source of pain is the self we've cast?
Regret creeps in like a shadow's touch,
A bitter twist of sorrow, too much to clutch,
As we chase approvals,
Leaving our spirit in confusion's grasp.
We seek forgiveness from the world outside,
Yet fail to find peace within, to coincide.

Why do we turn from the truth inside,
Rebelling against the quiet voice we hide?
In the territory of self-awareness,
Where clarity shines,
Why do we crave validation still,
From the world, from others,
to fill the void, so blind?
Why do we struggle to embrace our light,
And fight against the truth that can set us
right?
For in the end, rebellion is not a fight
without—
But a quiet war within the soul,
A journey to meet ourselves,
To strip away ego's hold.
So, I ask—who is the true *Rebel*—
The one who defies the world with fire,
Or the one who dares to face,
The truth that lies within, and rise higher?

Harmony

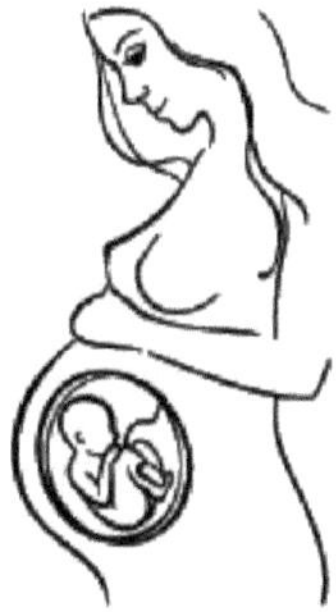

First cry that breaks the silence of night,
A fragile sound, yet so full of might.
A helpless wail, a newborn's plea,
A mother's heart finds its key.
The child arrives, an innocent call,
A promise of joy, to heal and enthrall.
In every tear and tender embrace,
The mother finds her strength, her grace.
Through pain's cruel grip, a silent bond,
The mother's love, tender and fond.
The child's warm hug, an unspoken prayer,
Healing each wound with a comfort rare.
As the child grows, in wisdom's bloom,
The mother learns to dispel all gloom.
In every need, in every cry,
She finds herself reaching, learning to fly.

In moments of doubt, in sleepless nights,
The child's laughter is true delight.
Through every step, both large and small,
They rise together, following the call.
For motherhood is not a single song,
But a symphony where both belong.
It's not a journey walked alone,
A path where two hearts are grown.
Together, they grow, side by side,
Through every ebb, through every tide.
A mutual dance, a sacred plea,
In the quiet, in the harmony.
So, Mother, with endless care,
Know your child's love is always there.
For in this bond, deep and true,
Both of you are born anew.
In this dance of life, where hearts align,
Mother and child, in perfect rhyme.
In the quiet rhythm of love's embrace,
They find their sacred space.
And through it all, this truth they see:
Mother and child, in perfect *Harmony.*

Special

At times, thoughts collide,
A quiet longing to feel admired,
To rise,
Amid the daily rush, we often miss
Subtle joys that soothe heart's abyss.
The sun ascends daily and paints the sky,
Yet each dawn brings a whisper, soft and shy.
The moon, too, glows with gentle grace,
A timeless marvel in night's embrace.

Velvet sheets may captivate the eyes,
Yet humble cotton draws us nigh.
A steaming cup of tea, a warming delight,
While water's simplicity brings pure respite.
Luxury calls, yet peace comes unbidden,
In moments of stillness, where calm is hidden.

No need for others to bind or prove,
When the heart knows its worth, serene and smooth.

The world feels vast, yet when we see,
Each moment holds a deeper key.
In simple things, the soul finds its place,
For these quiet treasures, we softly embrace.
No grand spark to light the way—
For we are *Special*, in our own quiet sway.

Flow Unbroken...

Bliss in a moment,
Fervor in a spark's embrace,
Patience woven through hours,
Pulse in arcs that swiftly race,

The arrival of destiny's breath,
The closing of days as light fades,
Seasons swirling in timeless dance,
Tireless toil through time's cascade.

Waiting through ages uncounted,
Perseverance of kindred souls,
Ascetic devotion across centuries,
Lore of millennia, bound in scrolls.

Fragments of time,
Scattered, yet one,
And rivers that carve
Through cosmic expanse,
Eternal, radiant,
Immaculate, love—
Remains, in *Flow Unbroken*...

Conspiracies of time

Time's gentle stirrings,
Soft, unseen,
Carried whispers of your presence,
Alive, ever in between.

The call of time's creases,
A subtle, pleading sigh,
Yet, in oblivion's haze,
I drifted, lost in its silent tide.

Countless springs,
Slipped like grains of sand,
Endless evenings of yearning,
Silent, unspoken, yet grand.

Today, my eyes met yours,
As if desires long unsaid,
Had finally found their resting place,
Time's wrinkles, gently spread.

In quiet dance of fate,
Distance unraveled, set free,
For love, though masked in absence,
Lives on, eternal as the sea.

Guided by the hands of time,
It reveals when least we see,
A truth beyond the surface,
Whispered in eternity.

For love, like time, is boundless,
A force beyond the mind,
And in its quiet conspiracies,
We find what was meant to bind.
Conspiracies of Time

Unyielding Hearts

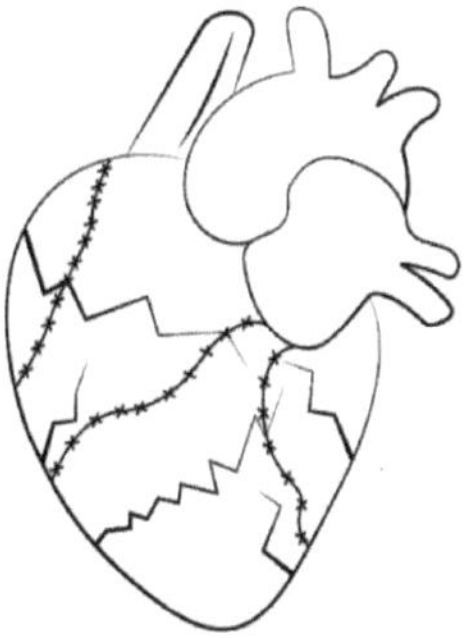

In silent gestures, I read your signs,
I am no puppet, bound by your lines.
The universe reflects its true form,
Yet I'm an unstable thread, torn and worn.
Where do I bind, where do I stay,
When the world shifts and pulls me astray?

Moments, affection so brief,
Why must I bloom, only to grieve?
In the storm of your wrath,
Burning so bright,
How do I worship, and make it right?
Is my endurance of your every frown,
The true measure of strength
That you've found?

Does my surrender, my quiet refrain,
Demand questioning, cause such pain?

I bow in love, my heart open wide,
Within me, a quiet strength resides.
I give you all, yet lose none of my own,
For in my soul, I stand full-grown.
Love is my offering, pure and true,
I am no weaker, just because of you.
My dreams are my own, my spirit unbroken,
In depths of my heart, a strength unspoken.
Through all the chaos, all that we've been,
It is this unwavering love that keeps me in—
Unyielding Hearts.

Soar High

Closed eyes, in stillness rest,
Lifted spirits, standing at their best.
Why cower in fear, bound by doubt?
What if you fall? It's part of the route.
Gravitation pulls, you won't be lost—
Rise again, no matter the cost.

Hold yourself, then rise anew,
For you've only fallen where dreams pursue.
The sky won't falter, nor the stars fade,
The blue awaits, for light to invade.
Why lament, or mourn the fall?
For you're destined, stand tall.

In silence you've watched,
From the sidelines, you've seen,
Let your actions bold, not serene.
Sigh, with unwavering might,
Spread your wings, soar to new height.

Fear not the fall, or trials you've known,
For within you lies a strength of your own.
So rise, unbroken, let your spirit fly—
Fear not, *Soar High*, reach for the sky.

Shuttlecock!

Step down from that fragile pedestal,
Leave behind that hollow dock,
The gleaming altar you revere,
Is but a mirage, a transient mock.
The cape of honor they offer,
Is a chain, gilded yet tight—
Meant to steal your dreams and light,
To drown your voice in endless night.

Do not beg for praise at their door,
Seeking approval with a lowered head—
Don't be that shuttlecock,
Tossed in the air, aimlessly led.

A sacrifice in silence,
For a world that won't understand,
Don't be the subtle cock,
A pawn in someone else's hand.

Spread your wings, unshackle your soul,
Rise from the depths where shadows lie—
Be the watchful hawk above,
With wisdom in your piercing eye.
For you were born to shape the skies,
To rule the wind, to blaze your way—
Do not bow to fleeting dreams,
But soar above the fray.

The world may try to cage your flight,
To clip your wings, to dim your might,
Remember, strength is never bound,
It rises, fierce, from the ground.
So don't be that *Shuttlecock*,
Don't be the Subtle Cock,
Be the Hawk—unfettered, unbroken,
And let your spirit forever be outspoken.

Canvas

From sorrow's abyss, creation blooms,
A phoenix rising from life's glooms.
The past, a shadow that softly fades,
The future, a mist where nothing stays.

Yet here and now, the present gleams,
A fertile ground for all your dreams.
A blank *Canvas* stretched wide and vast,
Not bound by the chains of future or past.

You are the artist, the brush is your will,
Each stroke a choice, each moment to fill.
Do not wait for fate to draw the line;
The masterpiece is yours to define.

The genie you seek is within your core,
Hidden beneath trials you abhor.
Sorrows, rejections—they are the spark,
Lighting the lamp within the dark.

When life shatters, don't despair,
Gather the shards with tender care.
Each piece a lesson, each crack a guide,
To the treasure that waits inside.

The past is a phantom, whispering lies,
The future an illusion in disguise.
But the present, ah, the present sings,
A symphony of boundless things.

Live now, breathe deep, and dare to dream,
Flow like water in life's rushing stream.
The unknown canvas was meant to be,
An endless space for your artistry.

So paint with courage, with colors bold,
Weave your story, let life unfold.
For destiny bows to those who create,
And within you lies the master of fate.

Ambition

Ambitions are a compass,
pointing us toward the unknown,
a force that drives us to dream,
to stretch, to strive.

But what is the summit
in a world without peaks?
A spherical existence
spinning in a cosmos
without a center,
where every top
is someone else's bottom,
and the chase circles endlessly.

The metaverse shifts, dimensions evolve—
today's crown, tomorrow's dust.
When the world rewrites its rules
and the goals you bled for fade,
what will remain of you?

Do not lose yourself in the mirage of success,
a flickering flame that offers no warmth.
Pause. Look around.
This journey was never meant
to be a race.

Know yourself.
Feel the earth beneath your feet,
the wind that carries your breath.
This moment, this present—
it is enough.

You are enough.
The joy lies not in the finish line
but in the footprints you leave,
the laughter, the pauses, the stories.

Stop.
Not forever, but long enough to see,
that life isn't a conquest,
but a kaleidoscope,
a dance,
a gift meant to be lived.

And at the core of it all,
beneath the striving and the dreams,
lies the truth of your journey—
Ambition.

Shine, my heart!

Time after time, it breaks!
In myriads of ways,
Crumbled, shattered, scattered—
a thousand fragments aflame,
consumed by a fire it kindled itself.

Yet, in the ashes of its ruin,
amidst the scattered remains,
tiny glimmers emerge,
like mica dancing in the sunlight.

In each shard, a defiant glow,
Prisms of hope,
this unruly, relentless heart of mine—
burned, broken,
and still, dares to *Shine*...

Penance

If it sustains the flame of my love alive,
let your enigmatic poison of passion linger.
I will endure the cost of loving the heartless,
and embrace this life of sacrifice,
for love, even unreciprocated,
a quiet devotion, I choose to bear—
My *Penance.*

Interludes

Electrons are knocked loose,
Semiconductors stripped of peace,
Impurities pressed into their veins,
Perfect sheets marred, reshaped,
All for the gift of conduction.
Why? Because even perfection
Bends to purpose,
Interludes of particles and impurities,
At play, for conductivity.

Organic tissues spun into threads,
Woven to shroud mortal frames.
We marvel at the beauty of the weave,
Yet stumble on the borders of prejudice,
Defining artistry by origins,
By the warps and wefts of bias.

Interludes of thread and thought,
At play, for exquisite artistry.

The gravity of silence,
The levity of sound,
Dance in an unseen duet.
Words, notes, vibrations —
They matter, but so does the void.
The pauses, the stillness between,
Give melody its soul.
Interludes of clefts and cadence,
At play, for a symphonic whole.

Forests of concrete or fertile green,
Fields, meadows, or barren moors,
Natural or forged by human hands,
All canvases paint their stories.
Colors of joy and shades of sorrow,
Born from the void,
Returning to it.
Stars blaze in vivid galactic hues,
Only to dissolve into infinite black.
Interludes of bright and gray pixels,
At play, for polished art.

Words, soft or sharp,
Spoken or swallowed,
Emotions unruly or steered,
Flow into verses.
In between lines,
in the spaces unsaid,
Meaning breathes,
A deliberate pause, a silent beat.
Interludes of thought and feeling,
At play, weaving poetry from life itself.

Catalyst

Be the spark that sets the change,
An agent in the cosmic range.
Unseen, yet vital in the tide,
A force through which transformations ride.

You bear the heat, the clash, the strain,
The moments steeped in joy or pain.
The bonds that break, the forms that shift,
You hold your ground, a silent gift.

The glory or the blame may fall,
On others who partake in all.
Yet you, unshaken, stay your course,
Detached from triumph, free of remorse.

Through every turn, through ebb and flow,
You guide the paths where reactions go.
Unmoved by praise, untouched by spite,
A quiet witness to the light.

And when it ends, the world anew,
You stand apart, as you always do.
Unconditioned, whole, and pure,
The soul of change, steady, sure.

Be that the *Catalyst*, strong and still,
Transform the world, bend fate to your will.
For though the storms may rage and flare,
You remain steadfast, aware.

Close to Divine—Electrons

Invisible whispers of ancient lore,
Once revered, their mysteries soared.
In silent awe, untouched they lay,
Until reason dawned to light the way.

Renaissance rose, ignorance fled,
Civilization wove its golden thread.
Science unveiled their hidden might,
Electrons ignited the dawn of light.

Parts of progress, humble and fair,
Givers of plenty when handled with care.
Yet in reckless hands, their force untamed,
Brought ruin swift, with none to blame.

They nurture, they guide, unseen yet profound,
Threads of connection the world spins around.
Waveforms shimmer, a soul's faint glow,
Bridging realms we may never know.

Turbines of power, disciplined and wise,
Driving the engines where humanity lies.
Detached from greed, yet ever aligned,
Electrons—eternal, divine, intertwined.

With every pulse, their truth refines,
Electrons, close to divine.

Vengeance

From enigmatic realms, it ascends in flames,
A resplendent inferno unyielding in its claim,
Scorching sinew, a spirit's despair,
Yearning for solace that lingers nowhere.

Horizons extend, desolate, grim,
Hatred's conflagration, fierce and dim,
Unbent by compassion, immune to reprieve,
A relentless torment none can deceive.

Vanity's hand, insidiously fed,
Justice starved, morality bled,
Resolve dismantled, courage displaced,
Humanity left forlorn, debased.

Upon the parchment of thought, a pyre
ignites,
A dirge for another's transgressing rites,
Yet why must you, in embers, fade?
A riddle through which wisdom wades.

This vehement blaze, tempestuous and dire,
Yearns for atonement to temper its ire,
Its echoes linger, both cruel and just,
Binding mortals to vengeance's thrust.

To quell this storm, to temper the fire,
A redemption sought in the heart's quagmire.
But in the ashes, unyielding and dense,
Lingers the shadow, eternal—*Vengeance.*

Replenish

Let time and distance weave their grace,
Annihilating all grudges,
Burning away the shadows of hurt,
Ill will and despair dissolve like dust,
Leaving behind only quiet spaces
Where healing may root.
From the rifts of our hearts,
New life arises, slow and steady,
Sprouting seeds of hope,
That bloom in the
nourishing soil of forgiveness.
In the depths of our souls,
A quiet renewal stirs,
Reconstructing what once was broken,
And weaving the threads of peace,
to *Replenish.*

Sublime!

Burdens of my day dissolve,
In the sanctuary of your thought.
Weights of accusations banish,
In solace your presence brought.

Anger and resentments fade,
Cradling in your embrace.
Emptiness haunting me dissipates,
Through truths that you illuminate.

Relentless trials of time recede,
As your essence intercedes.
In that union, all pain refines,
Transcending ache, to *Sublime*.

One more time...

May my love
obliterate the shadows of unlove,
unraveling the knots of pain
that scar your being.
May my love
flow, a gentle stream,
washing away toxicity,
each drop a balm to wounds deep.

May my love
heal you, piece by piece,
mending the fractures of your spirit.

May my love
embolden your heart,
to rise, unafraid, and place its faith,
One more time,
in those miracles of love—
Timeless, infinite, and true.

Keepers of Sleep

You, silent guardians of slumber,
Binding the sacred cycles with grace,
A quiet force, unseen yet profound.

You craft the cinema of the unconscious,
Untamed thoughts curled into reels—
Worlds we long to touch,
Stories we dare not live.

You stir laughter, coax out tears,
Unveiling truths we dare not face,
Revealing the fears that linger,
Yet offering strength where none existed.

In your shadows, nightmares rise—
Dark mirrors of our deepest selves,
Through them, clarity emerges,
Answers whisper from quiet depths.

"It never hurts here,"
Carroll's wisdom softly echoes,
For in your realm,
Pain fades into lessons,
Wrapped in gentle embrace.

Stewards of journeys untold,
You churn, you heal,
Guiding through the labyrinth of self,
Transforming sleep into a reflection.
You, *keepers of sleep—*
Dreams.

Festival of Light

In this harsh, unforgiving world you stand,
The unsullied fragrance, gentle and grand,
A bloom untouched by fate's cruel hand.

In the sharp notes of soprano,
You are the tender touch, soft yet firm,
A harmony where all notes affirm.

Amidst the roar of silence so deep,
You are the call that wakes from sleep,
A whisper that stirs the stillness to leap.

In the chaos of critique and blame,
You are the laughter, wild and tame,
A dance of irony, untamed by fame.

In depths of fate's design,
You are the light, scintillating,
A beacon, unwavering in its glow,
A *festival of light*,
Only mine.

Zebras losing stripes!

Evolution is inevitable, a force that drives,
Cosmos, the sun, moon, stars, all alive,
From species to civilizations, all have moved,
Changing, growing, for good, improved.
Yet in this age, we chase perfection,
An elusive name, in natural selection.
What led us to forget our ethos,
In universal design where truth echoes?

The stars, the moons, the sun's warm glow,
In their chaos, beauty flows,
Intelligent, precise, and captivating still,
Yet we chase ideals that blur our will.
Why must we digitize our nutrition, our skin,
Tweak every feature, as if we're less within?
Why the need for perfect cheekbones to rise,
Or flawless teeth, set in perfect lines?

Do we not see the beauty in speech,
Despite crooked fashion of teeth?
In laughter carefree, shedding false disguise,
Behind dusky skin, where real beauty lies.
In love received, no matter the frame,
No measure of weight can lessen its flame.
In service to others, with open heart,
Despite extra pounds, only kindness's part.

We're born in a way uniquely ours,
Our health is wealth,
Our care, our strength in these hours.
But why the race, the urge to reshape,
To cast aside what makes us great?
Why are we becoming
Zebras losing stripes,
Their very own identity, lost in hypes?

Antidote

Fear of the vast unknown,
Uncertain future's looming tone,
Gathered in a corner, tightly bound,
Illness and death in silence found.

Cause and effect, a tangled web,
Doubt arises where decisions ebb,
Uncertainty cloaks each thought and choice,
Inaction reigns, leaving no voice.

Why paint future in shades of night?
Why not face today with courage bright?
Why not embrace the present, clear and true,
And leave behind all fear that grew?

When answers seem distant or unclear,
Create your path with resolve sincere,
Unlock life's mysteries with your hands,
Through hard work, carve your own demands.

Let countless cosmic signs lead the way,
In wisdom's light, let doubts decay,
Through hard work, the soul will find,
A cure for fears that cloud the mind.
In the face of illness, despair, and strife,
For poisonous doubts that confide,
Hard work is the only *Antidote*,
Every effort, every stride.

Universal Processes

From atoms to matter, in silent pace,
To interactions, time can't erase.
Reactions ignite, energy whirls,
Cosmic dance, change unfurls.

Thoughts arise from endless flow,
Creation emerges, in radiant glow.
Matter shifts, like tides that wane,
Atoms return, to start again.

Camouflage

Why are we bestowed with this art to hide,
To conceal the truth and shadows abide?
Why flaunt a mask and glare,
Veiling what's real, and truth bare?

Why shelter joy behind sorrow's veil,
Concealing our laughter, though hearts sail?
Why not stand and proclaim, clear and true,
"I am happy, my spirit renewed"?

Why does a predator, silent and sly,
Blend in the dusk, beneath a darkened sky?
Why does a seed, in the quiet earth,
Tuck itself in, awaiting rebirth?

Flowers bloom in secret, shy and still,
While plants reach upward, against their will.

Why must time, in shadows, conceal,
What's destined to bloom, to stretch, to heal?

Why hide behind the velvet of night,
As if darkness alone holds our light?
Why does rage pulse through each living
thing,
As creatures and atoms in silence sing?

Is it fear, or a longing to blend,
To shield what's fragile, to defend?
Or is it simply that we seek to belong,
In a world where silence often feels wrong?
Why at all is there a rage,
For every species and particle to *camouflage*?

Ego's flame, Love's glow

Aura of aplomb, and flame of ego—
One who understands their difference,
Possesses the true courage of love.
The rest fade,
lost in their own effervescence.
Yet for me, there remains—
You, luminous, eternal, aglow!

Listen closely, it's a dream...

Listen closely, it's a dream—
A dream that I hold dear.
If you ever find it, bring it to me—
Tens of books, vibrant and alive,
with pages beautiful, fragrant,
And a cup bottomless, of warm tea,
Steaming gently in the quiet air.
Surround me with a peace so deep,
That no sound dares to stir.
Let only the soft murmur of turning pages
Resonate in the stillness of my mind.

Generational Music

Like riyaz that echoes from dusk until dawn,
Flaws illuminated, charts are drawn.
Why not follow the rhythm of compassion,
In generations so distant?

Generations rise like sound waves,
Why bind them to an octave?
Sweetness is not in a single refrain,
But in melodies that flow
through change's domain.

Rhythm, pitch, and syllables too,
Each carries a voice both old and new.
Traditions hold patterns, strong and clear,
Yet creation thrives when efforts are sincere.

It's not the tune that turns into discord,
But rigid rules that silence, ignored.
To grow, there must be room—
In harmony, unity finds its loom.

Without this shift, division takes root,
Bound by rules that stifle the pursuit.
Only in the dance of change and grace,
Can generations truly find their place.

Discipline

In battle's field, practice takes its form,
When restraint, like a storm, holds its norm.
Through rituals, character is shaped,
And with forgiveness, strength is draped.

From fear, emerges courage,
Through action, purpose finds rage.
In life's wild woods, vast and deep,
Know its expanse, and the trials we keep.

Patience, like the Nandi bull, strong and true,
Oh Nandini (girl), your form reflects what's
due!
Cast off the cloak of ego's disguise,
That stains and tarnishes soul's prize.

Merge the rhythm, let it align,
Bind the spine with discipline's sign.
Prepare with steadiness,
The heart and mind,
So that vision remains sharp,
And in focus, defined.

In all things, let the guiding force be clear,
Through every struggle, every tear.
The path to mastery, the journey's key,
Is found in one word–*Discipline.*

... In the grip of need

Inventions arise not from what we expect,
but from the silent force of what we need.
So too does knowledge, a steady current,
self-sustained, self-determined—
acquired not as a duty, but as a need.

We hear, "Learn from the creatures who serve,
even in their death."
Yet I ask, what if we take their lives
for our own sustenance,
and use their herds without thought?
We turn deaf to their pain,
and still, we consume,
because it is what we need,
and this is how they are bred.

The mighty sun, indifferent,
shines for all—
it doesn't play hide and seek.
Even when cursed, it casts its light,
without favor, without prejudice.

Immobile autotrophs,
silent in their giving,
ask nothing in return—
they offer shade, oxygen, life.
Had they chosen otherwise,
if survival demanded they withhold,
our existence would falter,
unsustained, ungrounded.

We aren't bound
by miracles or fantasies,
not by grace of unknown gods.
We stand firm on the axle of need,
able, stable,
our lives woven together
by the quiet threads of necessity,
held tight—
in the grip of need.

Paradox of Power

To gift the world
The sacred joy of motherhood,
You, bound by the inviolable thread of duty,
Were cradled in the lap of Mother Earth,
Your presence, a spell that dazzled,
Casting enchantment
With the pure radiance of your face.
As time unfurled its endless scroll,
The lightness of childhood faded,
Giving way to a weighty, responsible youth,
Like a silver moon, you blossomed—
Rising from the shadows
Of a world blind to your worth.

Even in the presence of light,
The claws of darkness stretched,
Hungry wolves roamed untamed,
And fate itself stood still,
Paused by the birth of a new star,
Emerging from the womb
Of night's deepest void.

In your innocence, you walked,
Unaware that after father and husband,
Another force would shape your destiny—
A power both tender and unyielding,
A force granted by your very being.
Caught in the labyrinth of existence,
You, one day, will slip away
From this fleeting world,
Yet not a single tear will trace your cheek,
For you are the silent bearer
Of every burden.

Like a crystal-clear cascade,
Ever flowing through
Deltas of murk and mud,
You merge with the vast ocean,
Attaining the liberation
That eluded you in life.
Once, your voice—raw and trembling—
Sought blessings,
But now, it speaks only in silence,
For it matters not if your words are heard,
For even in the shadow of oppression,
Your spirit remains unbroken.

You are the keeper of sorrow,
The silent river that absorbs the world's pain,
And still, you press forward—
The pulse that stirs creation into being,
The breath that ignites the flame of life.

This is the essence of womanhood—
A paradox woven with strength,
A quiet storm that shapes the world,
A force that births, nurtures, and endures,
A soul that carries the weight of the universe,
Yet asks for nothing in return.

You are the foundation, the rhythm,
The very soul of creation itself—
A living testament to the Paradox of Power.

The Fly and the Sty

Once upon a time, a fly,
Dreamed of living in a sty.
She thought it'd be a cozy spot,
But soon discovered it was a lot...

The bad people were in charge,
Workers aiming to make it large.
They planned to clear the garbage away,
Which left the fly in disarray.

"Oh no!" she thought, "I'll have my say!"
"I'll make them pay for this today!"
So, she rallied her fly brigade,
And hatched a plan with skills well laid.

But, alas, her efforts went to waste,
For the workers were swift, no time to waste!
With teamwork and brains, they cleared the mess,
Leaving the fly in deep distress.

And as the garbage finally disappeared,
All that was left was the fly's shattered cheer—
For her dreams of a sty had flown away,
In defeat, she buzzed, "I'll find a new place to play!"

The Beauty Bone Chronicles

When I was young,
I didn't know the term "beauty bone,"
It was just a mystery, far from my teen-zone.
But then, as I grew, my dear kith and kin,
Introduced me to this term, much to my chagrin.

"Beauty bone," they said, "It's all the rage!"
To get one, you must diet and turn the page
On butter, carbs, salt, and sugar galore,
For a body that's "perfect," you can eat no more.

In this fashion-obsessed, judgmental world,
If you're not "perfect," you're the joke unfurled.
So, I jumped on the diet train with glee,
Ignoring my parents who said, "That's not healthy, you see!"

Days went by, I became weak and frail,
Picking up a chair was now quite the tale!
I got thinner and thinner, bones barely in sight,
But still, no "beauty bone" made its debut that night!

Finally, I realized—what a dreadful mistake!
So, I decided to eat more, for goodness' sake.
A balanced diet and exercise too,
To regain my strength and feel like new.

One day, staring at the mirror with a sigh,
I suddenly jumped, my eyes grew wide!
There it was, in all its glory and tone—
Yes, my humble, sober beauty bone!

The High Heel Revolution

Everywhere you look, it's all about fashion,
Or, to put it simply, it's today's grand passion.
Everyone wants to look smart, you see,
Whether by hook, crook, or some new decree.

In this fashion-obsessed, self-conscious parade,
The goal is simple: fair, thin, and tall—never afraid.
Beauty salons, clothes, and shoes, oh my!
Become the reasons we sigh.

But short folks (like me) often face the jest,
Made fun of for height, never feeling their
best.
No longer do I stand on tiptoe just to be seen,
Nor feel small in a world that's so keen.

Why, you ask? What's this change I've found?
Well, my friends, it's nothing short of
profound—
A remedy has been launched, for both tall
and small,
And we all flock to it, strutting down the
hall.

Did you guess it yet? Oh, you're so wise!
Yes, it's the high-heeled shoes—what a
surprise!
Now, no matter how short, I stand tall with
pride,
And never again will I have to hide!

So here's to the heels that give us a boost,
Making tall folks and
Short folks feel equally spruced!
Fashion's now fair, and I'm standing tall—
Thanks to the heels, I can conquer it all!

Biology Blues

If you take three letters out of BIOLOGUS,
It becomes BOGUS—now that's no fuss!
Just think about the subject, if you dare,
When they force-feed this stuff to your brain,
Poor, unaware.

No wonderland to find, no magic in sight,
Just endless hours of cramming day and night.
You mug like a parrot, repeating with might,
Until your throat's sore and your words take
flight!

Tooth-cracking spellings, names you can't pronounce,
And no, they won't guarantee you an MBBS or an ounce—
Of sanity, that is, because the initial study's neat,
Plants and leaves, it all seems sweet.
But then—oh no!—the plot takes a turn,
You're off to study how the human body can churn.
And just when you think you're on the right track,
You feel your mind's about to crack!

Instead of learning, your brain takes a flight,
Escaping the planet, lost in the night.
Headed straight for the universe's dungeons,
Tone deaf to all summons!

So here's to biology, the subject we adore,
That leaves us wondering, "What's it all for?"
A subject so fun, yet full of strife,
But hey, at least it's never boring—right?!

A Salmon's Journey

Beneath the waters, you were born,
In the quiet depths, unattained.
Your childhood, a dance in the currents,
A world of wonder, where you swam carefree.
But as you grew, currents began to shift,
Peaceful waters, no longer a gift.

Oh, pathetic salmon!
From innocent fry to a gleaming prize,
You were "ready" now, in nature's eyes.
Your flesh, once untouched,
now sought to be caught,
A prize for those who waited, who taught.
Waters turned cold, the hunt began,
And you swam against tides, could never
outrun.

First, the safety you knew was taken away,
The freedom to glide, now subject to prey.
The predators circled, waiting for you,
And each turn you took, they grew in pursuit.
Oh, pathetic salmon! You swam so blind,
Not knowing the loss that waited behind.

As you grew in strength, your life became a race,
A fight for survival, a contest to face.
Your body, now fragile, was stretched and worn,
Each turn, a struggle, each choice, a thorn.
Oh, pathetic salmon! Your once-joyous song,
Now fades into silence, as you swim along.

And then came the river, its path ever steep,
A journey so harsh, the waters so deep.
The strength you had once used to rise,
Now drained from you, swallowed by the skies.
Oh, pathetic salmon! With each passing stroke,
You lost more of yourself—your spirit broke.

The waters grew darker, the currents did twist,
You swam and you fought, but something was missed.
The life you once held with freedom and grace,
Was now a battle you could not face.
Oh, pathetic salmon! No longer the same,
The world had consumed you,
your strength lost to fame.

And when you reached the end of your flight,
A place of darkness, the end of the fight,
No longer would you swim with ease,
Your life now taken, to satisfy their pleas.
Oh, pathetic salmon! In your final breath,
You gave all you had, in the face of death.

Oh, pathetic salmon! We must now see,
The fragility of your life, the cost of being free.
For each stage of your growth,
something was lost,
A piece of your soul, a heavy cost.

But what if, one day,
you chose to break free,
And let go of everything, just to be "me"?

Career Crisis

What to be, what to do,
The endless choice—
oh, where's the clue?
I sat and pondered, filled with dread,
Sipping water, staring ahead.
Should I be this, should I be that?
Or just stay home and nap like a cat?

Becoming a housewife seemed so fine,
Just ladles and wok, a daily grind.
Say goodbye to freedom and charm,
Trade it for cleaning, with no alarm.
The kids and husband, demands galore,
I'd lose my peace and maybe more!
Guilt would be my constant friend,
Where do my needs and wants end?

Wait! I could be a doctor, right?
Save lives, be kind, all day and night.
But imagine, a room full of germs,
I'd suffocate, my sanity would squirm!
What if I fail, what if they die?
Oh, the shame! I'd just want to cry.
I'd lose my temper in a flash,
And the hospital would be my crash!

Or... maybe a lawyer, sharp and quick,
Argue all day with words so slick.
Shouting, bargaining, with no rest,
A moral compass put to the test.
In front of the jury, I'd make my plea,
But would I be judged for just being me?
I'd lose my voice to endless chatter,
And still wonder if it even mattered.

Water running low, my mind in a whirl,
I couldn't decide between career or pearl.
So I put it off—what a wonderful plan!
Tomorrow I'll think, but today, I'll just tan.
Next morning, again, the water in tow,
I'll decide... or maybe I won't, who knows?

The Teenage Trials

So here we are, the age of 13 to 19,
They call it "teenage"—sounds kind of mean.
They say it's a perilous, wild ride,
Where hearts break free and run to hide.
Why it happens, no one can explain,
We just follow the crowd—it's all the same.

First, there's the pimple invasion, oh joy!
Cheeks and chin, now you're the teen decoy.
A helpful sign that you're growing fast,
"Hey, look at me! I'm not a kid, at last!"
New thoughts pop up—
Two, three thoughts, maybe four,
Climbing steep slopes, but who needs more?

They seem impossible, like a mountain too tall,
Yet somehow we try, and we stumble, then fall.

We cry for help—like dogs on a spree,
Barking at life, "Why's this happening to me?"
But hold on a minute, don't get too stressed—
Not everything's bad,
Some thoughts are still blessed.
What we need is a bit of bold flair,
To face it all with a wild teenage stare.
So, here's the deal—it's not all despair,
We just need to dare and take it from there.

Discovering Happiness

We often dwell
on what makes us sad,
Fixated on the cause,
forgetting to feel glad.
Happiness isn't something to invent,
It's something to discover.
Like water waiting in the earth,
It's found when we uncover its worth.

It's not owned by a smile alone,
But felt deeply, from the bone.
Those born to be happy
Don't dwell on the cobwebs,
They know joy and sorrow ebb and flow,
like threads.

Happiness and sorrow, they fall like rain,
Like herbs that grow in the sun and pain.

Every cloud has a silver lining, they say,
But patience is needed for it to play.
In times of sorrow, you may feel low,
But know that joy, like spring, will soon grow.
When happiness arrives,
don't greet it with doubt,
Celebrate its spirit, let it out!

It knows no limits, no end, no bar,
So why chase butterflies,
when you can raise a garden far?
Plant the seeds, tend with care,
Watch as happiness blooms everywhere.

Peace

In this small, four-chambered hall,
Reside joy and sorrow, both big and small.
Then comes the mind, the master of all,
Capable of solving, making sense of it all.
It holds the key to peace, a power so true,
The strength within you in all that you do.

Peace is the courage that flows from your
soul,
Patience and confidence complete you whole.
In the midst of chaos, we find our grace,
Peace becomes the center, our sanctified
space.
We feel its warmth, a soft, healing air,
Even in turbulence, peace lingers there.

Our freedom was won with a bloodied fight,
But peace is what carries us into the light.
Bringing peace may seem far and wide,
Yet silence and stillness help us inside.
Meditation and prayer, the paths we take,
To restore our balance and help us awake.

From parents to grandparents, the wisdom
stays,
Echoes of peace through the passage of days.
The chirp of a robin, the raven's call,
All remind us to seek peace above all.
In the morning, in the evening, in every mind,
Peace is the treasure, for all humankind.

Home Sweet Home

A house is just a structure, walls with a fence,
But a home is where love makes perfect sense.
It's a place where we gather, where hearts align,
Where we find comfort, and worries decline.

A house is a home, a safe retreat,
Where family comes together, where hearts meet.
In joy or sorrow, we share the ride,
Through highs and lows, with arms open wide.
Candles of hope are always aglow,
In a home where love and warmth flow.

A house is a home with sunlight so bright,
Where summer mornings feel pure and light.
Or winter's frost, a chilly embrace,
But within, we're safe, in this sacred place.
Every moment is lived with grace,
No worries, no haste—just peace in space.

A house is a home when friends are near,
Laughter and chatter we hold dear.
Even Mondays feel sweet, not a chore,
In a home, there's always room for more.

Home is more than walls or roof,
It's where love resides, where truth is proof.
It's not just shelter, but a place we belong,
A haven where hearts can sing their own
song.

The Blue Unknown

Above us lies the vast, blue sky,
Endless and unknown, yet so close, so nigh.
Where stars, the moon, and planets roam,
And castles of daydreams find their home.
Birds soar freely without a care,
And the horizon feels like it's always there.

Man's ambition to reach it, to touch the heights,
Is not so impossible, though it feels out of sight.

Yet the sky, with its messengers of rain or shine,
Shows no judgment, no decline.
It holds its head high, through storm or glow,
A quiet strength that we all know.

A shelter for all, without distinction,
It's we who are divided by outdated conviction.
The sky doesn't care for our feeble plight,
It just stretches onward, in endless flight.
It's where the kites dance, wild and free—
Yes, it's the blue unknown, where we long to be.

Willing to Succeed?

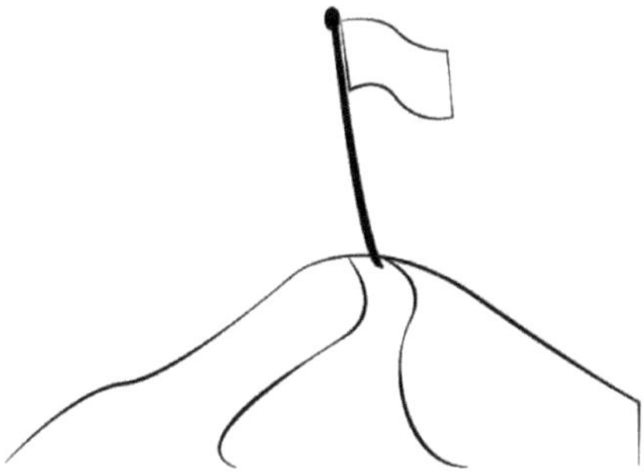

Dreams are gifts, from God above,
He knows you're perfect, worthy of love.
Success is within reach, only if,
You're willing to rise, face every rift.

Obstacles come, opportunities in disguise,
A test of your spirit, a chance to rise.
Judge yourself not by ease or grace,
By your courage to keep the pace.

Challenges shape you, make you strong,
The tougher the road, the more you belong.
With belief in your strength, your mind, your soul,
You'll find success is within your control.

Failures may come, but don't lose heart,
They are stepping stones, just the start.
Try again, and again, and again—
For success is not a destination,
It's the journey's gain.

Stay enthusiastic, remain optimistic,
Smile through the hardships, stay realistic.
The world will align, as you choose to
proceed,
With the right aptitude, you'll always succeed.

A Prayer

More and more, my heart prays—
Not for bones to beg, but for thanks to raise.
Here I stand, with gratitude deep,
For the guidance you've given, the promises
you keep.

Lord, you have shown me the way,
Awakening me with each new day.
I ask not for riches, fame, or gold,
But for the strength to keep my soul bold.

Grant me focus, patience, and love,
Guide me with your power from above.
Give me a pure heart, steadfast and true,
A heart that beats with strength anew.

Take pride away, let humility reign,
Let self-respect remain, free from disdain.
Help me stand firm, not lost in the crowd,
To walk my path with confidence, proud.

When I falter, untrue to my dreams,
Guide me in silence, or so it seems.
For I have chosen you, Lord, my guide,
In you alone, I choose to confide.

If I stray, lead me back to the light,
Let your presence be my might.
And if I remain stubborn,
Pull me by the ears,
Teach me my lesson,
But God, please stay near.

A rolling stone with no moss

A birth that bloomed,
with joy in the air.
A delicate soul,
soft beyond compare.

Bestowed upon parents,
with hopes shining bright,
a flower so pure,
a beacon of light.

Heavenly dreams wrapped
in her tiny frame,
the world looked on
with love, without shame.

But as she grew,
the hopes began to shift,
Her parents' desires,
a weight, a heavy lift.

They wished her to shine,
to soar, to be grand,
a moon in the sky,
with the world in her hand.

Love turned to demand,
expectations took root,
a sea of wishes,
that buried her truth.

Sweetened with poison,
expectations did rise,
clouding her skies,
souring her prize.

Her dreams grew dim,
her heart grew tight,
confined by the world,
no space left for light.

She ran through the race,
but could never win,
thoughts bound by "should,"
as she tried to fit in.

Morals and values,
taught as a chain,
trapping her soul,
stirring up pain.

She had to prove,
to conform, to obey,
silencing her doubts,
and clearing the way.

She learned to love,
without asking for more,
to turn negativity
into something pure.

But somewhere along,
she lost her own name,
her identity fading,
lost in the game.

Her small dreams drowned,
beneath the cost,
her hopes discarded,
her soul nearly lost.

She became a rolling stone,
tossed in the fray,
chasing expectations,
day after day.

No longer a flower,
just a stone,
drifting through life,
lost and alone.

Her roots have withered,
her spirit long tossed,
she is now a rolling stone,
with no moss.

First love

For so long, my dreams had been my only
guide,
Pushing me forward, consumed by my career,
Chasing success,
burying the doubts that I could never hide.
I studied, I fought,
determined to stand on my own,
Believing I could overcome every obstacle
with my will.
Yet, I was unprepared for the soft wave that
came,
That gentle force that stopped me in my
tracks—
A wandering soul, suddenly rooted at a
crossroad in life.

At that very moment, something inside me shifted,
A strange completeness blossomed in my femininity,
As his thoughts brushed against mine,
And in his gaze, I found myself.
My dreams, once uncharted,
now seemed clearer,
As blood surged in my veins,
And my fingers trembled
with the rush of adrenaline.

There, in that quiet, unexpected moment,
I realized love had happened,
Not through words, not through time,
But in the fleeting, unspoken glance,
The first unseen sight that captured my heart—
And in that instant, I knew:
Love had found me,
In the most unexpected way.

Writing Dilemmas

Every time I write,
My thoughts become a kite,
Ideas soaring, full of delight.
But, oh, what a mess! I can't decide,
Between what's wrong and what's right.

When I write a joke, I think it's fun,
Some laugh and laugh,
Others say, "You're done!"
Is it comedy or just absurd?
Maybe it's both, or just a blur.

Then I pour my heart in something deep,
Expecting sympathy, a love to keep,
But some call it devotional, a sacred plea—
While others ask,
"Is this your recipe for tea?"

What once felt clear, now turns to mush,
Some see it as art, others a rush.
I try and try, but all in vain,
This is my dilemma—such a pain!

One thought is joy, another is strife,
Trying to write makes me question my life!
Each word I pen,
Each thought I say,
Seems to get misinterpreted
In a numerous way!

So here I am, in a constant bind,
Trying to share, losing my mind.
If you see my words and think they're too far,
Just remember, I'm just being bizarre!

This is my dilemma, it's plain to see—
I write, I fumble, and just hope you agree!

Love Blossoms

Love blooms in endless tides
When you're away,
For in your absence,
My heart finds its way.
With each moment apart,
A soft unfolding,
Where your absence stirs my soul,
Gently molding.

Every breath I take
Aches with desire,
As the void you leave
Sparks an inner fire.

In silence
Where your presence is missed,
My love swells,
Infinite, in quiet bliss.

A devotion in conflict

O supreme archer,
though my heart longs to unite in your worship,
I find myself unable, my spirit adrift in disquiet.
O eldest son of Dasharath,
though I wish to bow my head in reverence,
My soul resists, caught in a tempest of doubt.

O lotus-eyed,
though my affection yearns to weep,
Tears do not fall,
for they are held captive by grief unspoken.

O Ram,
though I desire to witness your grace,
I cannot bear the thought of Vaidehi,
left alone in her fiery trial.

Virtue, they say,
belongs to both father and beloved,
Yet, why your father's honor
Only upheld in your exile,
While a pregnant wife
was left to suffer in the wilderness?
Shabari, Ahalya, and
the vanquished emperor of Lanka—
They too knew the weight of virtue and
sacrifice,
But still, I am left to wonder,
In my humble understanding,
Why must Sita endure the fire,
When your heart, too,
was wounded by loss?

Rescue me from this flawed intellect,
O Purushottam, in your infinite grace,
That I may engrave your name upon my heart,
And, though burdened with questions,
Find solace in your divine presence,
As you, the finest of the Raghu lineage,
Step into this world, and into my soul,
With answers only you can reveal.

Are you listening, Krishna!

Krishna, I've forgotten the path of love,
That once led me to you, my heart so true.
Lost in the chaos of fate's cruel hand,
Now, no song for you plays in this land.
No melody to call you near,
No rhythm to bring you here.

I am but a timid soul,
Too meek to raise my voice, to take control.
Yet, Krishna, where is your conscience so
bright,
Your wisdom, your Mahavidya's light?
You've sheltered a thousand queens with care,
And in this, I assume you're aware
Of the struggles women face each day,
So why are you blind to their dismay?

Are you waiting for complaints to arise,
Or offerings to open your eyes?
Why do you silently watch, so still,
As adharma spreads and takes its fill?

You came to reveal this truth,
Must we suffer sorrow to know your proof?
How many trials, how many tests,
Must I endure to prove my worth, my quest?
To show I'm worthy of your love,
To rise and shine as you would above?

O guardian of Draupadi's plea,
Rescue us—the humble, the lost, the broken,
we!
Do not delay, do not stay away,
Return to Earth with your wounded foot
today,
For your mark of suffering, so deep and true,
Will only heal once this pain is through.

Incarnate as Vamana,
Narasimha, or Parashurama,
Or wear the form of Kalki, so bold,
And walk among us, the stories untold.

Destroy the evil, the crooked, the dark,
O Sustainer of the world, ignite the spark.
O Vishnu, embodiment of grace,
Let injustice vanish, take its place.
Let your Sudarshan light the way,
And restore the balance, come what may,
That love and truth may reign again,
In this world, where we must mend.

Yet, the heart dares to love again

After the storms, after the pain,
When love has left its bitter stain,
The heart, though scarred, dares to dream,
To trust again, to let hope gleam.

Through tangled paths and whispered lies,
It seeks the truth beyond the skies,
For love, though lost, still softly calls,
And rises where the heart once falls.

Amid the cold, the dark, the drear,
There are those whose love is pure, sincere,
With steady hands and hearts that know,
They heal the wounds and help us grow.

Why does the heart dare love once more?
Because love is what it's meant for,
Without it, the soul would fade away—
Love is the breath that lights our way.

And so, we honor the heart's refrain,
The heart dares to love again.

A Polished Diamond

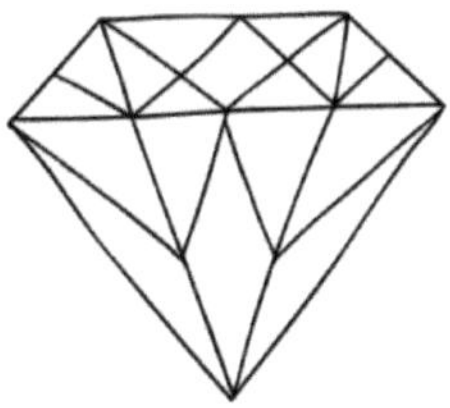

To cleanse, to heal, to truly shine,
It's not fate's hand, nor cruel design,
But the choice to let go, to surrender the past,
To unearth the brilliance, hidden at last.

Life will grind, it will shape, it will twist,
But it's not the storm that makes you persist.
It's the quiet surrender, the soft letting be,
Allowing the light to flow freely.

The tarnish of yesterday must fade,
The rough edges smoothed with steady blade.
A craftsman's touch, gentle, but sure,
Chisels away till your essence is pure.

It's not fate that molds, nor the weight of the years,
But the courage to shed, to face all your fears.
To let the light pour in, to fill every space,
To illuminate your soul with boundless grace.

For only when you choose to release,
What holds you back, will you find your peace.
And like a diamond, polished and bright,
You'll shine, you'll shine, in the fullness of light.

The Commitment Conundrum

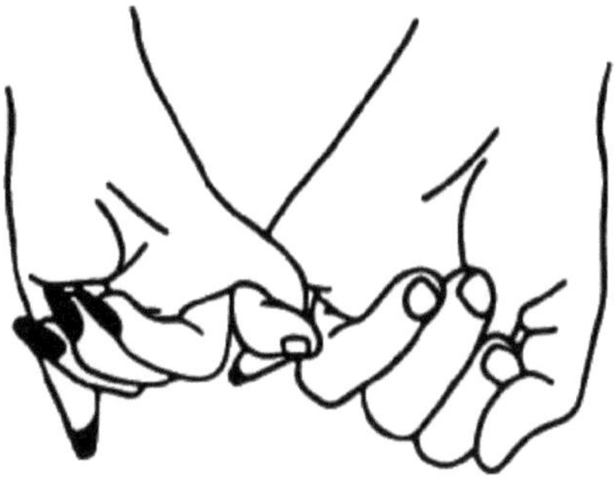

I love you a lot,
but there's a tiny hitch,
I'm great at the "now,"
But the future's a bit of a glitch.
You've definitely had your fill
Of the festival sweets,
But never once mentioned
The lack of the other treats!

I pour out love
Like a never-ending stream,
But commitment?
Well, that's more of a distant dream.

We’re in the moment,
full of sweet affection,
When it comes to forever...
Well, that’s a whole different direction!

So don’t worry,
We’re perfect in the "present" scene,
But as for long-term plans?
Let’s just keep it clean!

Sunshine at 9

Oh, how you shine at nine a.m.,
A golden call that wakes the heart—
Like September's bliss, so full, so rich,
In days of youth, when life's a start.

You stir the mind, you lift the will,
A whisper soft, yet clear and strong—
Like spring's first bloom at forty years,
You chase away what's held too long.

Your warmth, a bath of tender care,
That clears the dark, that melts the cold—
From cycles past, you bring relief,
And wash away the heavy old.

A thousand lotus bloom within,
In quiet realms, where dreams are spun—
Your rays ignite that secret fire,
And fill the heart with joy, undone.

O soft, sweet sunshine, pure and warm,
You guide our feet, you fuel our task—
In every beam, a call to rise,
To show up, work, and dare to ask.

Drenched in love, wrapped in care

Mumma, how did you raise us so?
With such simple joys, such love to show.
Back then, a tiffin was more than just a meal,
It was wrapped in care, in the warmth you'd
seal.

The oil that leaked from our boxes to the
books,
We didn't mind—oh, the little looks—
We knew it wasn't just food, you see,
It was love, in every bite, in every piece, it
would be.

Those chapatis drenched in the oil you fried,
Like your love, flowing deep inside.
We didn't fear cholesterol or the weight of it all,
Because your love was enough, standing tall.

You made life simple, you made it pure,
In every detail, love was sure.
We never complained, though we had so little,
Content with the joy, with the love in the middle.

Now, I pack their tiffin, so full of care,
But even silver foil gets a stare—
"Not oily food, Mum, it's unhealthy," they say,
Why can't you understand? Why act this way?

They want creativity in every bite,
Can't eat the same thing for two days, that's their plight.
I wonder how you did it, Mumma, so kind,
With all the love you gave, you shaped our minds.

Now, my kids want more—more variety, more flair,
And I'm left wondering how you did it with such care.
How did you blend the love and simplicity,
That we cherished, and still hold, with such humility?

You taught us to be grateful, no matter the fare,
Yet now, my children want more,
with tantrums thrown everywhere.
Mumma, you gave us the best of both worlds—
How did you manage it all,
while love blossomed and cradled?

Lie Foods

Son:
Mama, what's for Tiffin tomorrow?
What will I find to eat, what's in store?

Mama:
I'll make you pancakes, soft and sweet,
A breakfast treat, your favorite to eat.

Son:
And the next day, what will I have then?
Will it be different, or the same again?

Mama:
Tomorrow, I'll make you crepes so fine,
With chocolate syrup, Pumpkin mine!

Son (the next day, looking puzzled):
Mama, I have something to say,
Did you know,
You've been giving me "lie foods" each day?

Mama (astonished, her eyes wide):
Lie foods? What do you mean, my dear?
Tell me more, what's this you fear?

Son:
Day before yesterday, you promised me pancakes,
But when I opened my tiffin, there were "idlis" on my plate!
And yesterday, Mama, you said crepes with syrup so sweet,
But when I opened my tiffin, I found "cheela" to eat!
Mama, I have to be honest, this isn't quite right,
You've been giving me "lie foods" every bite!

Mama (chuckling softly):
Oh, my dear, you're so clever and bright,
It seems my promises got mixed up in the night.
I'll try harder, I promise, from now on to be true,
No more "lie foods" for you!

Illusion of Control

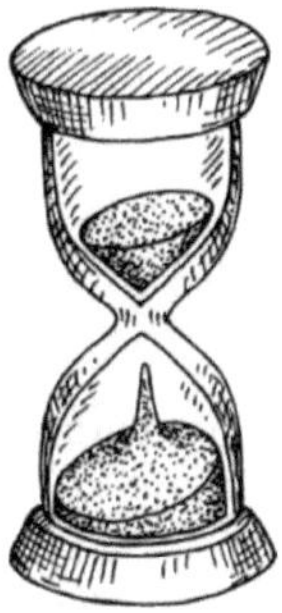

In the quiet stretch of events,
we lend time its power,
its vast, unwritten force,
its truth, its edge.

For it is we who shape its characters—
Change, ever shifting, ever flowing,
and Time, spun as endless space.
We, who breathe life into concept,
a flicker in the grand continuum,
a glitter among stars.

Yet, in our grasp, we boast of control—
We craft our strategies, plan our days,
earn and save for the rainy hour,
believing we steer this endless tide.
In the illusion that we hold the reins,
we forget how fleeting the grip really is.

But when it's time to reclaim that power—
When the pulse of existence demands it—
We choose to lay down our weapons,
abandon the charge,
forsaking what we've created.

Our thoughts, our views,
our theories and paradoxes—
they exist only in this sliver of time,
our fragile grip on what could be.
We, the makers of moments,
surrender our hold,
as if Time were ever truly ours.

In the end, are we the living?
Or are we merely dust and waves,
part of the tide,
prey to the change we've claimed to control?

We, who give dimensions to things,
and call it the passage of time.
In this vast space, do we not see?
The paradox, the fallacy—
that we back off, choose silence,
when the true power lies
in reclaiming what we've let go.

Real or Surreal

Where does true mastery of art reside?
In the strokes that mimic life with perfect stride,
In shapes and shades that breathe and move,
Where every detail's crafted, smooth?

Or does it live in realms not traveled,
In dreams and visions, bold and cold,
Where the mind dares wander, unconfined,
And reality bends, or redefined?

Is art the mirror of what we see,
Or does it weave a parallel world, that might be?
Does mastery lie in form and truth,
Or in the wild figments of random muse?

In life-like grace, or dreams unraveled—
Where does an artist's power channeled?
Is it in the real, or the surreal?
In what we touch, or what we feel?

Printed by Libri Plureos GmbH in Hamburg, Germany

9 789369 546626